# DID YOU KNOW?

## Rocky Mountain Series

### Photos and Text by Maresa Pryor-Luzier

**Front Cover: Elk Family on the Gallatin Range, Montana**


ISBN: 979-8-9856138-1-0

## The Rocky Mountains

The Rocky Mountains start in Canada and end in New Mexico inside the United States. They start at 9,000 feet at the timberline and go up to 14,000 feet.  This area is only for the toughest of the tough! Please support organizations like Rocky Mountain Network, Front Range Pika Project, and Tundra Guardians. Thank you!

## Dedication
To Faith & Harmony
My Inspiration!

Yellow-bellied Marmots

American Pika or Rock Rabbit

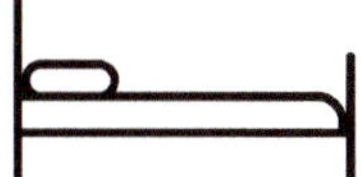

Which animal sleeps all winter?

Did you know the smaller pi-ka stores grasses like hay piles and stays active all winter?

While the larger mar-mot sleeps all winter known as hibernation.

WOW!

# Porcupine

How many quills does a por-cu-pine have?

**Up to 30,000**

What is a quill? Did you know they are sharp, hollow, and full of air, and rattle when shaken?

# Mountain Goat

# Why do Mountain Goats have spongy feet?

Did you know this helps them cling onto the mountainside?  Where they live is very steep and rocky.

Bighorn Sheep Ram
EWE

**What type of horns do Bighorn Sheep have?**

Did you know the ram's horns curl as they get older, and the females are much smaller?

Can you say ewe (U)?

# Elk

# What is an Elk?

Did you know they are the largest of the deer family and their antlers grow an inch a day?

The antlers can weigh up to 20 pounds and spread out to 4 feet.

That's BIG like you!

Alpine Forget-Me-Nots

Why are the alpine wildflowers so little?

Did you know growing low to the ground protects the flowers from the strong winds? SMALLER is better!

Sacramento Mountain Salamander

# What makes this salamander special?

Did you know they come from a family of climbing salamanders and use their tail to hold onto branches and rocks? Yes.

In addition, they are strong swimmers. Therefore, they are given the name "mini crocodiles." This one is only found in the Southern Rockies of New Mexico and nowhere else, making it very special.

# Rocky Mountain Birds

Steller's Jay/Subalpine

American Pipit/Alpine

Rosy Finch/Subalpine

How many birds do you see?

Did you know these 3 birds are all found at the top of the Rocky Mountains?

Where up top?

The area known as <u>subalpine</u> has trees, and the <u>alpine</u> does not, due to high winds, and it's very cold. Brrr …

Treetop

Grassy

Jagged

What kind of mountain tops can you see?

Did you know there are grassy, jagged, and treetop mountains? You can see a variety of mountain tops in the Rockies.

## Bristlecone Pine

**How old do you think this tree is?**

**Did you know this pine can live to be 5,000 years? How old is that?  When writing was invented.**

**CRAZY!**

**This tree may not be as old, but many years of strong winds have twisted the tree and its branches making it look old.**

Canada Lynx

**How does the lynx stay above the snow?**

Did you know the lynx's well-furred paws act as snowshoes? This keeps them on top of the deep snow.

## Red
## Fox

**What does a fox do when it's afraid?**

Did you know a fox will grin? Yes! Also, by laying low this clever fox can stay out of trouble.

# Grizzly Bear

Black Bear

**What is the difference between a Grizzly Bear and a Black Bear?**

Did you know a Grizzly bear is brown?  It has a hump on its back, dished face, and smaller ears than a Black bear.

What they both have in common is they sleep in dens during the winter months.

What's a den? A cave or underground space.

What do mountain goats, pikas, foxes, as well as birds, all have in common?

Did you know all living things need a place to live? The Rocky Mountains provide a home, food, and water for wildlife and their young for future generations.

The mountains are a place with strong winds. They are covered by snow in the winter but have green meadows in the summer. Next time you see the Rocky Mountains, you will know what lives there . . .

Published worldwide, Maresa Pryor-Luzier has studied and photographed the natural world for most of her life. She was raised in Sarasota, Florida and now resides in New Mexico with her husband, Sadie the dog, a few kitties, miniature donkeys, and horses.

She speaks on photography, nature, and conservation. Her photo credits include magazine and books such as National Geographic, Ranger Rick, National Wildlife, and Audubon. Also check out her *"Wetland Series."*

Please let Maresa know what you thought about *Did You Know? Rocky Mountain Series* by leaving a short review on Amazon or your preferred online store. It will help other parents and children find her book. Also feel free to contact her with any questions via webpage or social media.

Thank you!

For more information: https://www.maresapryorluzier.com
Facebook: https://www.facebook.com/mpluzierphotography
Instagram: https://www.instagram.com/mpluzier
Twitter: https://www.twitter.com/mpluzier